Is it...?

hard or Soft

Vic Parker

Heinemann

Little Nippers

H **www.heinemann.co.uk/library**
Visit our website to find out more information about **Heinemann Library** books.

To order:
☎ Phone 44 (0) 1865 888066
▤ Send a fax to 44 (0) 1865 314091
▣ Visit the Heinemann Bookshop at www.heinemann.co.uk/library to browse our catalogue and order online.

First published in Great Britain by Heinemann Library, Halley Court, Jordan Hill, Oxford OX2 8EJ, part of Harcourt Education.
Heinemann is a registered trademark of Harcourt Education Ltd.

Editorial: Jilly Attwood and Claire Throp
Design: Jo Hinton-Malivoire and bigtop, Bicester, UK
Models made by Jo Brooker
Picture Research: Rosie Garai and Sally Smith
Production: Séverine Ribierre

Originated by Dot Gradations
Printed and bound in China by South China Printing Company

ISBN 0 431 174024 (hardback)
ISBN 978 0 431 174020 (hardback)
08 07 06 05 04
10 9 8 7 6 5 4 3 2 1

ISBN 0 431 174075 (paperback)
ISBN 978 0 431 174075 (paperback)
08
10 9 8 7 6 5 4 3

British Library Cataloguing in Publication Data
Parker, Vic
Is it hard or soft?
620.1'126
A full catalogue record for this book is available from the British Library.

Acknowledgements
The publishers would like to thank Gareth Boden for permission to reproduce photographs.

Cover photograph reproduced with permission of Gareth Boden.

The publishers would like to thank Annie Davy for her assistance in the preparation of this book.

Every effort has been made to contact copyright holders of any material reproduced in this book. Any omissions will be rectified in subsequent printings if notice is given to the publisher.

Contents

This teacher wants to make a display of **hard** and **soft** things.

4

What can
the children
find at home?

5

Hunt for something hard

Something in this dressing-up box
is hard, like a table ...

Super stylish sunglasses!

Search for something soft

What feels soft and snuggly?

Some warm, woolly clothes.

Exploring toys

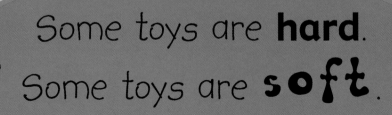

Some toys are **hard**.
Some toys are **soft**.

But which are which?

Stacking and shaping

Hard blocks are brilliant for building high.

Soft plasticine is perfect for making models.

Art test

Is the tip of a pencil soft?

Is the tip of a paintbrush hard?

Trying hats

tap, tap!

Here are some hard hats.

tap, tap!

What would you wear them for?

Everyday items

What's in the bathroom?
A soft sponge and towel ...

and a soft, squeezy tube of toothpaste.

Squish!

Soft surprise

Can you guess what is inside this hard mould?

Classroom display

soft things

Top marks for the treasure hunt.

hard things

Index

The end

Notes for adults

The *Is it . . .?* series provides young children with a first opportunity to examine and learn about common materials. The books follow a boy and girl as they go on a treasure hunt around their house to find items with contrasting textures. There are four titles in the series and when used together, the books will encourage children to express their curiosity and explore their environment. The following Early Learning Goals are relevant to this series:

Creative development
Early learning goals for exploring media and materials:
• explore colour, texture, shape, form and space in two or three dimensions
• begin to describe the texture of things.

Knowledge and understanding of the world
Early learning goals for exploration and investigation:
• investigate objects and materials by using all of their senses as appropriate
• show curiosity, observe and manipulate objects
• describe simple features of objects
• look closely at similarities, differences, patterns and change.

This book introduces the reader to a range of everyday items that are hard or soft. It will extend young children's thinking about familiar objects and enable them to talk expressively about different materials. The book will help children extend their vocabulary, as they will hear new words such as *display* and *stylish*. You may like to introduce and explain other new words yourself, such as *solid* and *squashy*.

Follow-up activities
• Suggest your child plays a 'sorting' game. Help them to divide their toys into 'hard' and 'soft' piles.
• Encourage children's ability with numbers by helping them to find ten hard things and ten soft things around the house.
• Build something with hard blocks such as wooden shapes, blocks or stickle bricks. Then make a model using soft playdough or plasticine.

24